Discovering

Deer

by Melvin and Gilda Berger

SCHOLASTIC INC.

New York Toronto London Auckland
Sydney Mexico City New Delhi Hong Kong

ISBN 978-0-545-24436-7

Copyright © 2010 by Melvin & Gilda Berger

All rights reserved. Published by Scholastic Inc.
SCHOLASTIC and associated logos are trademarks
and/or registered trademarks of Scholastic Inc.

12 11 10 9 8 7 6 5 4 3 2   10 11 12 13 14 15/0

Printed in the U.S.A.   40
First printing, September 2010

Photo Credits:

Cover: © John Cancalosi/Ardea; Back Cover: © Steven Kazlowski/Peter Arnold, Inc.; Title Page: © Manfred Danegger/
photolibrary; Page 3: © Chris R. Sharp/Photo Researchers, Inc.; Page 4: © Robert Kohlhuber (RF)/Getty Images; Page 5: ©
Biosphoto/Cahez Fabrice/Peter Arnold, Inc.; Page 6: © Paula Cobleigh/Shutterstock; Page 7: © James Stachecki/Animals
Animals; Page 8: © Andy Rouse/Nature Picture Library; Page 9: © Hans Reinhard/Corbis; Page 10: © Frans Lanting/
Corbis; Page 11: © imagebroker (RF)/Alamy; Page 12: © WILDLIFE/photolibrary; Page 13: © blickwinkel/Alamy; Page 14:
© Leonard Lee Rue III/Photo Researchers, Inc.; Page 15: © Hans Reinhard/Photo Researchers, Inc.; Page 16: © T.J. Rich/
Nature Picture Library

Deer live in the forest.

Deer eat grass.

What is this deer eating?

Sometimes they eat leaves.

Are deer ears bigger than your ears?

Deer have big ears.

Big ears catch every sound.

Male deer grow antlers.

Ouch! Antlers can hurt.

Deer can run fast.

They can jump far, too.

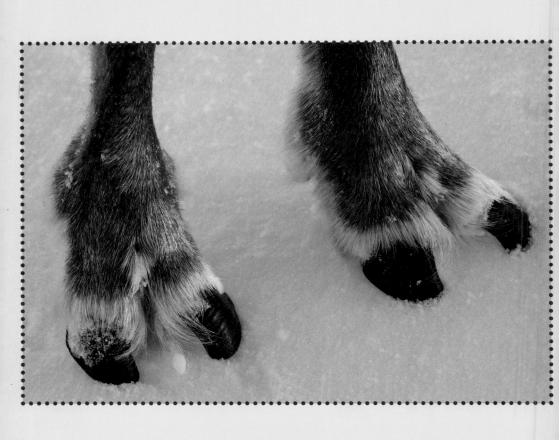

Each foot has two big toes.

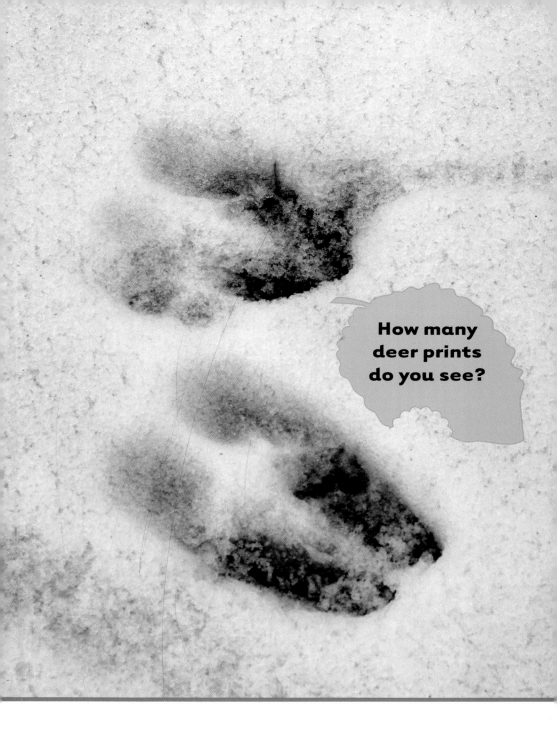

See the tracks in the snow.

Do baby deer have spots?

A mother deer cares for her baby.

Shh! The baby is going to sleep.

Ask Yourself

1. Where do deer live?
2. What do deer eat?
3. Do all deer have antlers?
4. Can deer jump?
5. Who cares for a baby deer?

You can find the answers in this book.